Grandmother Remembers

Family Recipes

Grandmother Remembers

Family Recipes

Conceived and written by Judith Levy
Designed and illustrated by Judy Pelikan

A Welcome Book

Stewart, Tabori & Chang, Publishers,
New York

Thanks to all
the Grandmothers who contributed to this book. J. L.

Edited by Marya Dalrymple
Text copyright © 1984 by Judith Levy
Illustrations copyright © 1984 by Pelikan Inc.

Distributed by Workman Publishing Company
1 West 39th Street, New York, New York 10018

Printed and bound in Japan.

*Sprinkled with love
And garnished with care,
Prepared with my heart
For generations to share.*

With love for _____

From _____

Date _____

Contents

A Wish for "Good Eating" Around the World

In our family we say _____

Afrikaans: Eet lekker
Arabic: Bel hana wel shafa
Bulgarian: Dobur apetit
Chinese: Ching che
Danish: God appetit
Dutch: Eet smakelijk
English: Good Eating
Eat Hearty
Hearty Appetite
Enjoy!
Finnish: Hyvää ruokahalua

French: *Bon appétit*
German: *Guten Appetit*
Greek: *Kahlee ohrexee*
Hawaiian: *E 'ai ho'oma'ona*
Hebrew: *B'tei avon*
Hungarian: *Jó étvágyat*
Irish: *Bain taithneamh as do bhéile*
Italian: *Buon appetito*
Japanese: *Itadakimatsu*
Korean: *Mat itke chapsuseyo*
Norwegian: *Velbekomme*
Polish: *Smacznego*
Portuguese: *Bom apetite*
Rumanian: *Pofta buna*
Russian: *Preyatnovo appetita*
Spanish: *Buen provecho*
Swahili: *Karibu mezani*
Swedish: *Varsågod*
Turkish: *Istahiniz acik olsun*
Welsh: *Archwaeth dda i chi*
Yiddish: *Es gezunterheyt*
Zulu: *Nginifisela kudla lokumnandi*

A Thought to Share

No matter how simple the meal,
No matter how lavish the spread,
We always expressed our thanks
Through the meaningful words that we said.

In our family, before we ate _____

_____

_____

_____

_____

_____

_____

_____

Meals were a time when _____

_____

_____

_____

_____

_____

_____

_____

_____

_____

_____

He who has fed
a stranger
may have fed an angel.

Spread
the table
&
contention
will cease.

A
NEW
BROOM
SWEEPS
CLEAN

Kitchen Wisdom

My favorite kitchen saying is _____

_____

Love is sweet but better with bread.

An apple a day keeps the doctor away.

A WATCHED POT NEVER BOILS

Black earth gives white bread

FOR EVERY POT THERE'S A COVER.

Recollections

Our family's food heritage comes from _____

_____

When I was young, my favorite food was _____

_____

My least favorite food was _____

In the kitchen, I used to help _____

_____

The job in the kitchen I liked most was _____

_____

The job I liked least was _____

_____

We usually ate dinner at _____

On Sundays we _____

_____

_____

I learned to cook at the age of _____

The first dish I ever made was _____

_____

I got the most help in the kitchen from _____

The table manners I taught my children were _____

_____

_____

14

When it came time to do the dishes _____
_____
_____

My favorite kitchen gadget is _____
I'm still old-fashioned about using _____
_____
_____

My favorite kitchen color is _____
Today I most like to prepare _____
_____
_____

Today my favorite foods are _____
_____
_____

My least favorite food is _____
_____

For breakfast I like _____
_____
_____

I enjoy snacking on _____
_____
_____

Grandmother Harrell's Spoon Bread

This southern dish is great served with creamed dishes or simply with lots of butter.

2 cups milk
4 eggs, separated

½ cup corn meal
½ teaspoon salt

Preheat the oven to 300°. Generously butter an ovenproof glass bowl.

In a saucepan, heat the milk but do not boil it. Beat the egg yolks slightly, then stir into the milk until blended. Add the corn meal and cook over low heat until thickened. Remove from the heat.

In a bowl, beat the egg whites with the salt until stiff. Fold into the corn meal mixture. Pour the batter into the prepared bowl and bake for 1 hour, or until the bread is golden brown.

To serve, spoon the mixture directly from the bowl onto plates.

Refrigerate any leftovers overnight, then, for breakfast, slice the bread, dip it in egg batter, fry it up, and serve with lots of syrup.

Serves 4 to 6

Wilhelmina Harrell

Breads

Jams

&

Jellies

Recipes for Breads, Jams & Jellies

A family favorite _____

_____

Ingredients and directions _____

_____

_____

_____

_____

_____

_____

_____

_____

_____

_____

_____

_____

_____

_____

_____

The person who loved this most _____

Recipes for Breads, Jams & Jellies

A family favorite _____

_____

Ingredients and directions _____

_____

_____

_____

_____

_____

_____

_____

_____

_____

_____

_____

_____

_____

_____

_____

The person who loved this most _____

Recipes for Breads, Jams & Jellies

A family favorite _____

_____

Ingredients and directions _____

_____

_____

_____

_____

_____

_____

_____

_____

_____

_____

_____

_____

_____

_____

_____

_____

_____

The person who loved this most _____

Recipes for Breads, Jams & Jellies

A family favorite _____

_____

Ingredients and directions _____

_____

_____

_____

_____

_____

_____

_____

_____

_____

_____

_____

_____

_____

_____

_____

The person who loved this most _____

Grandma Patty's Vegetable Beef Soup

4 large beef short ribs
1 can (10 to 12 ounces) beef bouillon or broth
1 pound fresh tomatoes, peeled, seeded, and chopped, or 1 large can (35 ounces) peeled whole tomatoes, coarsely chopped
2 celery ribs, coarsely chopped
2 carrots, scraped and coarsely chopped
2 medium leeks, cleaned and sliced
1 medium onion, chopped
½ pound mushrooms, sliced
1 teaspoon dried basil
1 garlic clove, minced
A few sprigs fresh parsley, chopped
2 unpeeled zucchini, diced
⅓ cup medium barley
Salt and pepper to taste

The day before the soup is to be served, boil the short ribs in 4 quarts of water with the bouillon for 1 hour. Remove the short ribs and refrigerate the broth and the ribs separately overnight. The next day, skim the fat off the broth. Remove the meat from the ribs, cube it, and add it to the broth. Add all of the remaining ingredients except the zucchini and barley.

Boil the soup, uncovered, for 1 hour. Cover partially, reduce the heat to low, and simmer the soup for several hours. One hour before serving add the barley and zucchini. Season with salt and pepper.

This soup is always best when made at least one day ahead of serving, or as many as three days ahead. Do not freeze the broth.

Serves 4 to 6

Patty Goebel

Soups
&
Stews

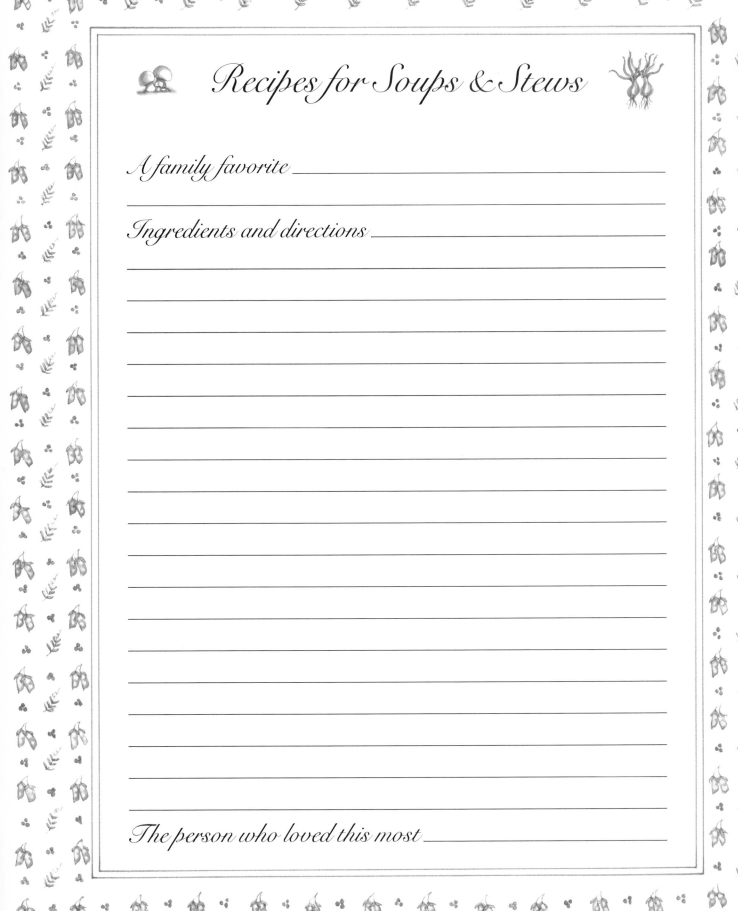

Recipes for Soups & Stews

A family favorite _____

_____

Ingredients and directions _____

_____

_____

_____

_____

_____

_____

_____

_____

_____

_____

_____

_____

_____

_____

_____

_____

The person who loved this most _____

Recipes for Soups & Stews

A family favorite _____

_____

Ingredients and directions _____

_____

_____

_____

_____

_____

_____

_____

_____

_____

_____

_____

_____

_____

_____

_____

_____

_____

The person who loved this most _____

Recipes for Soups & Stews

A family favorite _____

_____

Ingredients and directions _____

_____

_____

_____

_____

_____

_____

_____

_____

_____

_____

_____

_____

_____

_____

_____

_____

The person who loved this most _____

Recipes for Soups & Stews

A family favorite _____

_____

Ingredients and directions _____

_____

_____

_____

_____

_____

_____

_____

_____

_____

_____

_____

_____

_____

_____

_____

The person who loved this most _____

Nonni's Swedish Meat Balls

Vegetable oil
2 large onions, chopped
3 beef-flavored bouillon cubes
1 cup boiling water
1 cup dried bread crumbs
2 pounds lean ground beef
1 egg
A pinch of sugar
Salt and pepper to taste

In a skillet, heat 2 tablespoons of oil and saute the onions until
light brown. Dissolve the bouillon cubes in the boiling water.
Pour the bouillon over the bread crumbs.
In a bowl, combine all of the ingredients and mix well.
Shape the mixture into small balls and fry the balls in oil until
cooked through and lightly browned.

Serves 6 to 8

Anna Östblom

Poultry
Fish & Meat

Recipes for Poultry, Fish & Meat

A family favorite _____

_____

Ingredients and directions _____

_____

_____

_____

_____

_____

_____

_____

_____

_____

_____

_____

_____

_____

_____

_____

_____

The person who loved this most _____

Recipes for Poultry, Fish & Meat

A family favorite _____

_____

Ingredients and directions _____

_____

_____

_____

_____

_____

_____

_____

_____

_____

_____

_____

_____

_____

_____

The person who loved this most _____

Recipes for Poultry, Fish & Meat

A family favorite _____

_____

Ingredients and directions _____

_____

_____

_____

_____

_____

_____

_____

_____

_____

_____

_____

_____

_____

_____

_____

The person who loved this most _____

Recipes for Poultry, Fish & Meat

A family favorite _____

_____

Ingredients and directions _____

_____

_____

_____

_____

_____

_____

_____

_____

_____

_____

_____

_____

_____

_____

_____

_____

The person who loved this most _____

Grandma Endler's Pan Gravy

*This gravy never fails —
it's as good with a roast leg of lamb
as it is with a Thanksgiving turkey.
It works with a crown rib roast,
veal roast, or simply a plain
roast chicken.*

For each 1 cup of pan gravy, you will need:

Drippings from a roast
2   tablespoons fat (add melted butter or margarine if there is not enough fat from the roast)
1   cup liquid (composed of stock, canned broth, or a bouillon cube dissolved in 1 cup water, preferably from a cooked vegetable)
2   tablespoons flour

1   large onion, finely chopped
Salt and pepper to taste

Remove the roast from the roasting pan and let it firm up before carving. Pour off and reserve the fat from the pan, leaving 2 tablespoons of fat and the browned particles in the pan. Over high heat, add the liquid to the pan and stir, breaking up the browned bits that cling to the bottom of the pan.

In a large saucepan, heat the reserved fat and saute the onion over low heat until lightly browned. Add the flour and stir until the mixture bubbles. Remove from the heat.

Pour the liquid and the particles from the roasting pan into the saucepan. Stir together over moderately high heat until the gravy boils, about 1 minute. Season with salt and pepper and strain into a gravy boat.

Anne Endler

Sauces
&
Gravies

Recipes for Sauces & Gravies

A family favorite _____

_____

Ingredients and directions _____

_____

_____

_____

_____

_____

_____

_____

_____

_____

_____

_____

_____

_____

_____

_____

The person who loved this most _____

Recipes for Sauces & Gravies

A family favorite _____

_____

Ingredients and directions _____

_____

_____

_____

_____

_____

_____

_____

_____

_____

_____

_____

_____

_____

_____

The person who loved this most _____

Recipes for Sauces & Gravies

A family favorite _____

Ingredients and directions _____

_____
_____
_____
_____
_____
_____
_____
_____
_____
_____
_____
_____
_____
_____
_____

The person who loved this most _____

Recipes for Sauces & Gravies

A family favorite _____

_____

Ingredients and directions _____

_____

_____

_____

_____

_____

_____

_____

_____

_____

_____

_____

_____

_____

_____

_____

The person who loved this most _____

Grandma Pagano's
Stuffed Shells Marinara

½ teaspoon vegetable oil
12 ounces jumbo macaroni shells
2 pints ricotta cheese
8 ounces mozzarella cheese, cubed
1 egg
1 teaspoon chopped parsley
½ teaspoon salt
Pepper
Grated Parmesan cheese
Marinara Sauce (recipe below)

Preheat the oven to 325°. Bring 3 quarts of water to a boil and add the shells for 6 to 8 minutes, stirring occasionally until partially cooked. Do not allow the shells to become soft. Drain and set aside to cool. In a bowl, combine the remaining ingredients, except the Parmesan and marinara sauce, and fill the cooked shells with this mixture. Spread ¼ of the marinara sauce on the bottom of an ovenproof rectangular baking dish. Arrange the stuffed shells in a single layer over the sauce. Pour the remaining sauce over the shells and sprinkle with the Parmesan. Bake for 30 minutes, or until the sauce is bubbling hot. Serve immediately with hot bread and a green salad.

Marinara Sauce

2 tablespoons vegetable oil
1 medium onion, chopped
1 garlic clove, minced
1 large can (35 ounces) crushed tomatoes, or
   1 can (35 ounces) whole tomatoes, crushed
1 teaspoon chopped fresh parsley
1 basil leaf
½ teaspoon of oregano
Salt and pepper to taste

In a large saucepan, heat the oil and saute the onion and garlic until golden brown. Add the remaining ingredients and 1 cup of water. Simmer, uncovered, over low heat until thick, 20 to 30 minutes.   Makes about 1 quart

Serves 4 to 6

Gloria Pagano

Eggs, Pasta
&
Cheese

Recipes for Eggs, Pasta & Cheese

A family favorite _____
_____

Ingredients and directions _____
_____
_____
_____
_____
_____
_____
_____
_____
_____
_____
_____
_____
_____
_____
_____
_____

The person who loved this most _____

Recipes for Eggs, Pasta & Cheese

A family favorite _____

_____

Ingredients and directions _____

_____

_____

_____

_____

_____

_____

_____

_____

_____

_____

_____

_____

_____

_____

_____

The person who loved this most _____

Recipes for Eggs, Pasta & Cheese

A family favorite _____

_____

Ingredients and directions _____

_____

_____

_____

_____

_____

_____

_____

_____

_____

_____

_____

_____

_____

_____

_____

_____

The person who loved this most _____

Recipes for Eggs, Pasta & Cheese

A family favorite _____

_____

Ingredients and directions _____

_____

_____

_____

_____

_____

_____

_____

_____

_____

_____

_____

_____

_____

_____

_____

_____

The person who loved this most _____

Grandmother Prole's Scalloped Potatoes

2 potatoes per person, peeled and sliced ¼ inch thick
All-purpose flour, sifted
Salt
Pepper
Butter
Milk

Preheat the oven to 350°. Generously butter a casserole dish.
Arrange a layer of the potatoes in the bottom of the casserole.
    Dust the layer with flour, season liberally with salt and pepper,
    and dot with butter.
Continue layering in this way until you have filled the casserole.
Pour milk over the layers until it comes halfway up the sides of the
    casserole. Dot additional butter over the top and bake until the
    potatoes are tender and the top is golden brown and crusty,
    about 1 hour.

Alice Wolcott Prole

Salads
& Vegetables

Recipes for Salads & Vegetables

A family favorite _____

_____

Ingredients and directions _____

_____

_____

_____

_____

_____

_____

_____

_____

_____

_____

_____

_____

_____

_____

_____

_____

The person who loved this most _____

Recipes for Salads & Vegetables

A family favorite _____

_____

Ingredients and directions _____

_____

_____

_____

_____

_____

_____

_____

_____

_____

_____

_____

_____

_____

_____

_____

The person who loved this most _____

Recipes for Salads & Vegetables

A family favorite _____

_____

Ingredients and directions _____

_____

_____

_____

_____

_____

_____

_____

_____

_____

_____

_____

_____

_____

_____

_____

_____

_____

_____

The person who loved this most _____

Recipes for Salads & Vegetables

A family favorite _____

_____

Ingredients and directions _____

_____

_____

_____

_____

_____

_____

_____

_____

_____

_____

_____

_____

_____

_____

_____

_____

The person who loved this most _____

Grandmother Anne's Peach Crumb Cobbler

6 to 8 peaches, blanched, peeled, stoned, and sliced
Sugar
Cinnamon
1 cup sugar
1 cup all-purpose flour
1/2 teaspoon salt
1 teaspoon baking powder
1 egg
2 tablespoons sweet butter

Preheat the oven to 350°
In a buttered pie plate, arrange thick layers of the sliced peaches.
    Sprinkle generously with sugar and cinnamon.
In a mixing bowl, sift together the sugar, flour, salt, and baking
    powder. Add the egg and mix with your hands until the
    mixture is crumbly. Sprinkle the crumbly mixture over the
    peaches and dot with the butter.
Bake until the crust is browned, about 40 minutes.
Serve with heavy cream or ice cream.

Serves 6 to 8

Anne R. Stone

Cookies
Cakes & Pies

Recipes for Cookies, Cakes & Pies

A family favorite _____

Ingredients and directions _____

_____

_____

_____

_____

_____

_____

_____

_____

_____

_____

_____

_____

_____

The person who loved this most _____

Recipes for Cookies, Cakes & Pies

A family favorite _____

_____

Ingredients and directions _____

_____

_____

_____

_____

_____

_____

_____

_____

_____

_____

_____

_____

_____

_____

_____

The person who loved this most _____

Recipes for Cookies, Cakes & Pies

A family favorite _____

_____

Ingredients and directions _____

_____

_____

_____

_____

_____

_____

_____

_____

_____

_____

_____

_____

_____

_____

_____

_____

The person who loved this most _____

Recipes for Cookies, Cakes & Pies

A family favorite _____

_____

Ingredients and directions _____

_____

_____

_____

_____

_____

_____

_____

_____

_____

_____

_____

_____

_____

The person who loved this most _____

Good wishes are what count the most,
Not what's in the cup.
So choose what makes you happiest,
Let's toast and "Bottoms up!"

Grandmother Johnson's Party Punch

2 pints ripe strawberries, hulled, or 2 pouches
  frozen strawberries, thawed
½ cup superfine sugar
2 bottles (each 32 ounces) cranberry juice
  or white grape juice
2 cans (each 6 ounces) frozen lemonade
  concentrate, thawed
1 quart chilled sparkling water

In a large bowl, combine the strawberries,
  sugar, and 1 bottle of the juice. Cover and
  let stand at room temperature for 1 hour.
Strain the mixture through a fine sieve into a
  punch bowl, pushing the fruit through with
  the back of a wooden spoon.
Stir in the lemonade concentrate. Add the
  remaining bottle of juice and the sparkling
water. Before serving, add a block of ice.
If you prefer a punch with punch, substitute 2
  bottles of Rosé wine (each 25.4 ounces)
  for the juice.
As a festive winter holiday touch, freeze
  holly in a ring mold filled with water and
  use the ring of ice in the punch bowl. Or,
  in summer, freeze strawberries in the mold.

Makes 3 quarts

Dotty Johnson

A Toast!

Recipes for a Toast

A favorite punch _____
_____

Ingredients and directions _____
_____
_____
_____
_____
_____
_____
_____
_____
_____
_____
_____
_____
_____
_____
_____

The person who loved this most _____

Recipes for a Toast

Another special beverage _____

_____

Ingredients and directions _____

_____

_____

_____

_____

_____

_____

_____

_____

_____

_____

_____

_____

_____

_____

_____

_____

The person who loved this most _____

If they gave out a blue ribbon
This recipe would win it.
He said it's his favorite
And there's lots of love in it.

Grandfather's Favorites

Grandfather's favorite recipe _____

_____

Ingredients and directions _____

_____

_____

_____

_____

_____

_____

_____

_____

His favorite snack _____
_____

His favorite hot drink _____
_____

His favorite cold drink _____
_____

His favorite dessert _____
_____

For breakfast he _____
_____

For his birthday I _____
_____

Photograph

For Company

When company comes for dinner
It's very important to know
That the food will be really tasty
And that everything looks "Just so."

A Menu I Can Count On

_____

_____

_____

_____

_____

A favorite for company _____

_____

_____

Ingredients and directions _____

_____

_____

_____

_____

_____

I always plan the menu _____

_____

_____

I set the table _____

_____

_____

Before dinner I often serve _____

_____

_____

A dessert I can depend on is _____

_____

_____

The parties in our home are noted for _____

_____

_____

Grammy Gamble's Chocolate Cake

4 squares (1 ounce each) semi-sweet
   baking chocolate
½ cup boiling water
1 cup shortening
2 cups sugar
4 eggs, separated
1 teaspoon vanilla extract
2½ cups sifted cake flour
1 teaspoon baking soda
½ teaspoon salt
1 cup buttermilk

Preheat the oven to 350°. Butter and flour
   three 8- or 9-inch cake pans.
Melt the chocolate in the boiling water. In a
   bowl, cream the shortening and sugar until
   light and fluffy. Add the egg yolks one at
   a time, beating well after each addition.
   Mix in the vanilla and the chocolate.
Sift the flour with the baking soda and salt.
   Add the dry ingredients alternately with
   the buttermilk to the chocolate mixture, beating until smooth.

Beat the egg whites until stiff and fold into
   the batter. Pour into the prepared pans
   and bake for 35 to 40 minutes, until a
   toothpick comes out clean. Let cool before
   frosting.

Chocolate Icing

3 ounces cream cheese, softened
½ cup milk
4 cups confectioner's sugar
½ teaspoon salt
½ teaspoon cinnamon
4 squares (1 ounce each) semi-sweet
   chocolate, melted

Using an electric mixer, combine the cream
   cheese, milk, sugar, salt, and cinnamon. Add
   the chocolate and beat until fluffy. If the icing
   is too thick, add more milk, a teaspoon at a
   time.

Makes about 2¼ cups

Serves 8 to 10

Annie Gamble

Birthdays

My Birthday

My birth date is _____

My favorite birthday meal as a child was _____

_____

_____

The guests at my birthday parties were usually _____

_____

_____

My best birthday party ever was at the age of _____

At that party we _____

_____

_____

When I turned "Sweet Sixteen" _____

_____

_____

_____

The best present I ever received was _____

_____

_____

_____

The present I most wanted but never got was _____

_____

_____

_____

Today I celebrate my birthday by _____

_____

_____

_____

On my birthday the family always _____

_____

_____

_____

_____

_____

_____

_____

My Favorite Birthday Recipes

My favorite cake _____

_____

Ingredients and directions _____

_____

_____

_____

_____

_____

_____

_____

_____

_____

_____

_____

_____

_____

_____

_____

_____

_____

_____

Another birthday favorite _____

_____

Ingredients and directions _____

_____

_____

_____

_____

_____

_____

_____

_____

_____

_____

_____

_____

_____

_____

_____

_____

_____

_____

_____

_____

Special Family Birthdays

Name _____

Birthday _____

Relationship _____

Photograph

Name _____

Birthday _____

Relationship _____

Photograph

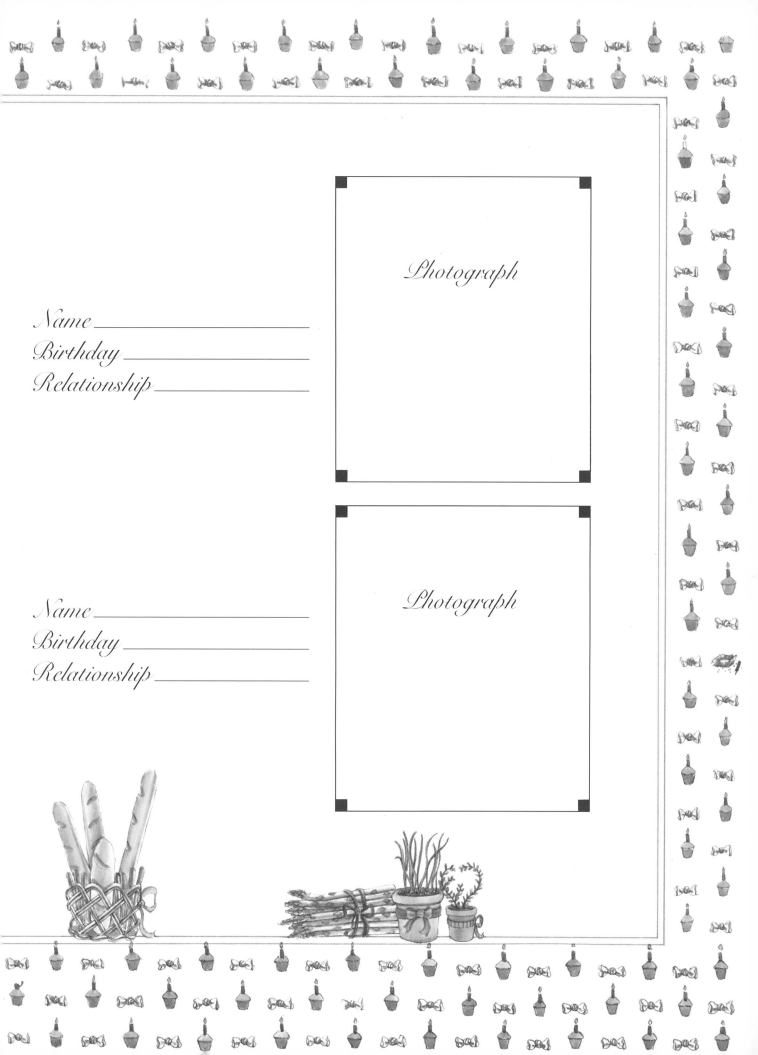

Name _____

Birthday _____

Relationship _____

Photograph

Name _____

Birthday _____

Relationship _____

Photograph

These special holiday dishes,
Prepared so lovingly,
Are rooted in remembrance
And family history.

Grandmother Armstrong's Cranberry-Strawberry Relish

2 pounds cranberries, rinsed
2 cups strawberry jam
1 cup sugar

Place the cranberries in a saucepan. Add water to cover and bring to a boil. Cover and cook for 5 minutes. Add the jam and sugar and cook until thick, 5 to 8 minutes. Chill before serving. You can make this relish well in advance of your holiday celebration.

Makes about 1 quart

Nan Armstrong

Holidays

Spring

Holiday _____

Date _____

We celebrate this holiday by _____

_____

_____

_____

A favorite holiday recipe _____

_____

_____

Ingredients and directions _____

_____

_____

_____

_____

_____

_____

_____

_____

_____

_____

Another holiday favorite _____

_____

_____

Ingredients and directions _____

_____

_____

_____

_____

_____

_____

_____

_____

_____

_____

_____

_____

_____

_____

_____

_____

_____

_____

_____

_____

_____

Summer

Holiday _____

Date _____

We celebrate this holiday by _____

_____

_____

_____

A favorite holiday recipe _____

_____

Ingredients and directions _____

_____

_____

_____

_____

_____

_____

_____

_____

_____

_____

*Another holiday favorite*_____

_____

*Ingredients and directions*_____

_____

_____

_____

_____

_____

_____

_____

_____

_____

_____

_____

_____

_____

_____

_____

_____

_____

Fall

Holiday _____

Date _____

We celebrate this holiday by _____

_____

_____

_____

A favorite holiday recipe _____

_____

Ingredients and directions _____

_____

_____

_____

_____

_____

_____

_____

_____

Another holiday favorite _____

_____

Ingredients and directions _____

_____

_____

_____

_____

_____

_____

_____

_____

_____

_____

_____

_____

_____

_____

Winter

Holiday _____

Date _____

We celebrate this holiday by _____

_____

_____

A favorite holiday recipe _____

_____

Ingredients and directions _____

_____

_____

_____

_____

_____

_____

_____

_____

_____

_____

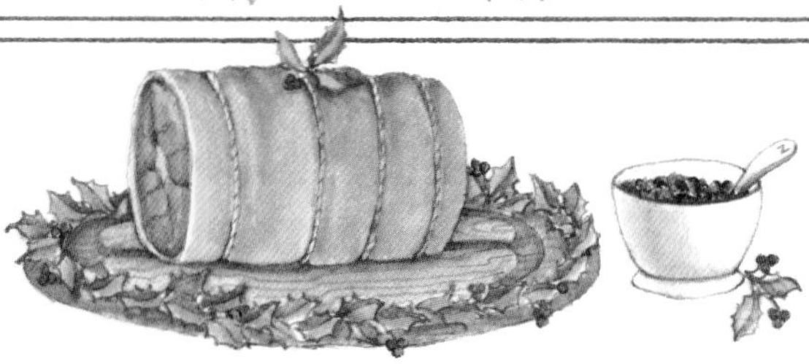

Another holiday favorite

Ingredients and directions

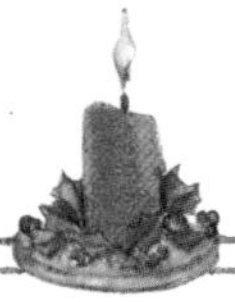

Holiday Photographs

Photograph

Photograph

Photograph

Photograph

Photograph

Photograph

Photograph

Photograph

When you're down and feeling blue
And your eyelids start to droop,
Nothing feels quite as good
As Grandmother's "Chicken Soup."

Bubbe Privin's Chicken Soup

1 4- to 5-pound chicken, quartered
3 carrots, scraped
1 small sweet potato, peeled
4 celery ribs with leaves

1 large onion, peeled
1 small parsnip, scraped
A few sprigs fresh dill
Salt to taste
1 box (8 ounces) of very thin egg noodles

Place the chicken pieces, vegetables, and dill in a large kettle and add water to cover. Cover the pot and bring the water to a boil over high heat. Skim the top of the broth, lower the heat, salt liberally, and simmer, covered, for 2 hours.

Remove the chicken and vegetables to a bowl and set aside to cool. Pour the soup through a strainer. When cool enough to handle, slice the carrots and return to the broth.

Remove the chicken from the bones and add it to the broth. Discard the remaining vegetables and the chicken bones. Salt to taste.

Just before serving, cook the noodles in a separate pot. Drain and add them to the hot soup.

Any leftover soup may be refrigerated, but be sure to skim the broth before reheating. This soup also freezes well.

Makes 4 to 6 quarts

Dina Privin

Loving Cure-alls

My favorite cheer-up recipe is _____

_____

_____

Ingredients and directions _____

_____

_____

_____

_____

_____

_____

_____

_____

_____

_____

_____

_____

I think this recipe makes you feel better because _____

_____

_____

_____

"Hand in the Cookie Jar" Stories

I still remember the time I got caught _____

_____

_____

_____

_____

I've never told anyone about the time I didn't get caught _____

_____

_____

_____

I once ate so much that I never again liked _____

_____

_____

_____

_____

*When I think of the word "diet" I*_____

_____

_____

_____

_____

*If nobody's looking, I can always eat one more piece of*___

_____

_____

_____

*The family always laughs about the time*_____

_____

_____

_____

_____

_____

_____

_____

Handy Hints from My Own Kitchen

Your Own Family Recipes

Here are recipe pages
For you to fill in too,
So future generations may treasure
This gift from me and you.

_____

_____

_____

_____

_____

_____

_____

_____

_____

_____

_____

_____

_____

_____

_____

_____

_____

Your Own Family Recipes

_____

_____

_____

_____

_____

_____

_____

_____

_____

_____

_____

_____

_____

_____

_____

_____

_____

_____

_____

_____

_____

_____

Your Own Family Recipes

Your Own Family Recipes

Your Own Family Recipes

Your Own Family Recipes